Practical
Fast Pasta

p^3

This is a P³ Book
First published in 2003

P³
Queen Street House
4 Queen Street
Bath BA1 1HE, UK

ISBN: 1-40540-938-X

Printed in China

NOTE

Cup measurements in this book are for American cups.
This book also uses imperial and metric measurements. Follow the same units
of measurement throughout; do not mix imperial and metric.
All spoon measurements are level: teaspoons are assumed to be 5 ml, and
tablespoons are assumed to be 15 ml. Unless otherwise stated,
milk is assumed to be whole milk, eggs and individual vegetables such as potatoes
are medium, and pepper is freshly ground black pepper.

The nutritional information provided for each recipe is per serving or per person.
Optional ingredients, variations, or serving suggestions have
not been included in the calculations. The times given for each recipe are an approximate
guide only because the preparation times may differ according to the techniques used by
different people and the cooking times may vary as a result of the type of oven used.

Recipes using raw or very lightly cooked eggs should be
avoided by infants, the elderly, pregnant women, convalescents,
and anyone suffering from an illness.

Contents

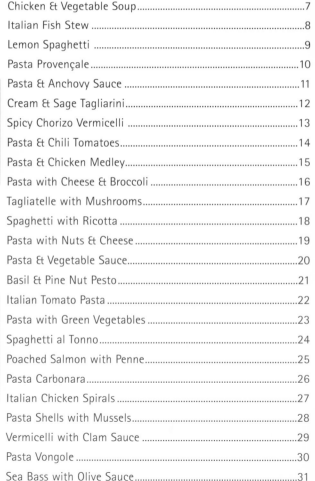

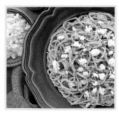

Introduction

Pasta is the perfect fast food. Not only is it so easy and quick to cook, but it can be stored ready and waiting in a wide variety of shapes, sizes, and colors to be turned into a mouthwatering meal in a matter of minutes. This delicious food is infinitely versatile, and can be combined in a delightfully simple way with a whole range of ingredients, from fresh vegetables and herbs to pantry staples such as canned fish, bottled olives, and nuts. Pasta is a healthy, lowfat food, and is an excellent source of complex carbohydrates, which fuel the body with slow-release energy. It also provides a useful supply of protein.

Choosing pasta

There are very many different types of pasta, but they basically fall into five separate categories:

Long, round pasta This includes the most familiar type, spaghetti, which is also available dried, in mixed packs of green (spinach), red (tomato), and plain. It also includes the finer spaghettini, and bucatini, which is like spaghetti only hollow. The very fine pastas are also included here. In order of increasing fineness, they are: vermicelli ("little worms"), capellini ("fine hair"), and capelli d'angelo ("angel hair"), which invariably come in "nests." Generally, these sorts of pastas are best served with a delicate olive-oil based sauce or a light cream sauce to keep the strands well-lubricated and separate. However, the more robust spaghetti and bucatini can carry bulkier, richer sauces.

Long, ribbon pasta The most well-known of this kind of pasta is probably tagliatelle. Fettuccine is a thicker, narrower version, traditionally with egg added, while pappardelle is wide with wavy edges. Other ribbon pastas include linguini, trenette, and the fine tagliarini. The thicker ribbon pastas are ideally suited to heavy sauces based on egg, cheese, or cream.

Flat sheet pasta This is basically lasagna, which comes in rectangular sheets with either straight or wavy edges.

Lasagnette is a narrower version. Dried lasagna does not require precooking when used in the traditional baked dish.

Short tubular and shaped pasta Short-tube pasta includes penne (quill shapes), plus the traditional macaroni and the ridged rigatoni. Cannelloni are thicker, longer pasta tubes for stuffing. Other pasta shapes include farfalle (butterflies), fusilli (spirals), conchiglie (shells), and

lumaconi (ears), or the smaller version, orecchiette. Chunkier tubes, such as penne and macaroni, are ideal for meat sauces or in baked dishes, while other shaped pastas go well with vegetable sauces and are attractive in pasta salads. Pastina refers to tiny pasta in different shapes, such as acini di peppe (peppercorn-shaped), farfallini, ditalini, and stellini, which are often used in soups.

Filled pasta Ravioli—those familiar frilled "pillows"—can be stuffed with meat, cheese, vegetables, or fish. Ring-shaped tortellini are available ready made, either fresh or dried. To avoid overwhelming the flavor, stuffed pasta is best served simply, with melted butter or oil and/or a little grated Parmesan, or with a simple tomato sauce.

Commercially produced fresh pasta is quick to cook but can vary in quality, and the finer strand or ribbon pasta is easily overcooked. Good-quality dried pasta mostly gives a superior result, and still only takes a few minutes to cook.

Useful utensils

There are a small number of tools and utensils that are invaluable for preparing pasta dishes:

Large, deep, heavy-bottomed pan with lid This pan is essential: it needs to hold a large quantity of water and have enough room for it to circulate around the pasta.

Large, deep, heavy-bottomed skillet A quality skillet is ideal for cooking pasta sauces quickly, especially if it can hold the cooked pasta as well—and it saves on cleaning time, since ingredients are less likely to stick to the pan.

Large colander with handles You need an easily held colander large enough to accommodate a hefty amount of pasta (to serve four people) for draining and shaking.

Pasta tongs These are useful for lifting and draining smaller quantities of strand pasta.

Skimmer This is ideal for lifting and draining stuffed pasta so that it remains intact.

Food processor This will save on time and effort spent preparing ingredients and making mixtures for sauces.

Swivel potato peeler This is the perfect tool for making Parmesan cheese shavings the quick and easy way.

Cooking pasta

Cook pasta in a large pan with plenty of fresh water. Allow 5 cups water to 4 oz/115 g pasta. Bring the water to a rolling boil, then add a little salt—about 1½ teaspoons per

5 cups. Add the pasta, feeding long pasta gradually into the water as it softens, and stir well. Put on the lid and return to boiling point, then uncover once boiling. Stir at frequent intervals while cooking. Test to see whether the pasta is cooked by removing a piece with a fork and biting into it. If it is properly cooked, it should be

tender but still firm to the bite (al dente). If cooked pasta is to be used in a baked dish, slightly undercook it. Tip it immediately into a colander to drain (or use a skimmer for stuffed pasta), shaking it once or twice but leaving a little water on it to prevent it from sticking together. For pasta salads, rinse the cooked pasta under cold running water, drain, then toss in a little olive oil.

Here are suggested guidelines for pasta cooking times:

Fresh, unfilled pasta:	2–3 minutes
Fresh, filled pasta:	8–10 minutes
Dried, unfilled pasta	10–12 minutes
Dried, filled pasta	15–20 minutes

Note: Whole-wheat pasta takes longer to cook; refer to the instructions on the individual package.

Pantry staples

You can keep the following ingredients in your pantry to make impromptu pasta sauces or simple seasonings in double-quick time. Flavored olive oil, such as chili, garlic, basil, or other herb oils, can add a boost to pasta, while balsamic vinegar gives a distinctive sweet-and-sour flavor. Dried herbs are particularly useful, like oregano, thyme, rosemary, and bay leaves. Black peppercorns are a must for pepping up pasta, as are dried chili flakes. Tomato paste and garlic paste are essential. Canned tuna, anchovies, salmon, and baby clams combine well with pasta. Canned tomatoes, beans, and pimientos are invaluable, and so are black olives, capers, and sun-dried tomatoes. Pine nuts, walnuts, and slivered almonds can come in handy too. Frozen peas and corn are good freezer staples.

KEY	
	Simplicity level 1–3 (1 easiest, 3 slightly harder)
	Preparation time
	Cooking time

Brown Lentil & Pasta Soup

In Italy, this soup is called *Minestrade Lentiche*. A *minestra* is a soup cooked with pasta; here, farfalline, a small bow-shaped variety, is used.

NUTRITIONAL INFORMATION		
Calories 225	Sugars 1g	
Protein 13g	Fat 8g	
Carbohydrate . . . 27g	Saturates 3g	

 5 mins   20–25 mins

SERVES 4

I N G R E D I E N T S

4 slices lean bacon, cut into small squares

1 onion, chopped

2 garlic cloves, crushed

2 celery stalks, chopped

1¾ oz/50 g farfalline or spaghetti, broken into small pieces

14 oz/400 g canned brown lentils, drained

5 cups hot ham bouillon or vegetable bouillon

2 tbsp chopped fresh mint

1 Place the bacon in a large skillet together with the onion, garlic, and celery. Dry cook for 4–5 minutes, stirring, until the onion is tender and the bacon is just beginning to brown.

2 Add the pasta to the skillet and cook, stirring, for about 1 minute, to coat the pasta thoroughly in the oil.

3 Add the brown lentils and the bouillon to the skillet and then bring the mixture to a boil. Lower the heat and simmer for 12–15 minutes, or until the pasta is tender.

4 Remove the skillet from the heat and stir in the chopped fresh mint.

5 Transfer the soup to warm soup bowls and serve immediately.

COOK'S TIP

If you prefer to use dried lentils, add the bouillon before the pasta and cook for 1–1¼ hours, until the lentils are tender. Add the pasta and cook for another 12–15 minutes.

Chicken & Vegetable Soup

This satisfying soup makes a good lunch or supper dish, and you can use any vegetables that you have at hand. Children will love the tiny pasta shapes.

NUTRITIONAL INFORMATION

Calories	185	Sugars	.........5g
Protein	........17g	Fat	...........5g
Carbohydrate	...20g	Saturates	.......1g

5 mins 15–20 mins

SERVES 6

INGREDIENTS

12 oz/350 g boneless chicken breasts

2 tbsp sunflower oil

1 medium onion, diced

1½ cups carrots, diced

9 oz/250 g cauliflower florets

3¾ cups chicken bouillon

2 tsp dried mixed herbs

4½ oz/125 g small pasta shapes

salt and pepper

TO SERVE

grated Parmesan cheese (optional)

fresh crusty bread

1 Using a sharp knife, finely dice the chicken, discarding any skin.

2 Heat the oil in a large pan and quickly sauté the chicken and vegetables, until they are lightly colored.

3 Stir in the chicken bouillon and the dried mixed herbs. Bring the soup to a boil and then add the small pasta shapes. Return to a boil, then cover the pan and simmer for 10 minutes, stirring the soup occasionally to prevent the pasta shapes from sticking together.

4 Season with salt and pepper to taste and sprinkle with Parmesan cheese, if using. Serve with fresh crusty bread.

COOK'S TIP

You can use any small pasta shapes for this soup—try conchigliette, ditalini, or even spaghetti broken up into small pieces. For a fun soup for children, you could add animal-shaped or alphabet pasta.

Italian Fish Stew

This robust stew is full of Mediterranean flavors. If you do not want to prepare the fish yourself, ask your local fish store to do it for you.

NUTRITIONAL INFORMATION

Calories	236	Sugars	.........4g
Protein	........20g	Fat	...........7g
Carbohydrate	...25g	Saturates	.......1g

🕐 5–10 mins   ⏱ 20 mins

SERVES 4

I N G R E D I E N T S

2 tbsp olive oil

2 red onions, finely chopped

1 garlic clove, crushed

2 zucchini, sliced

14 oz/400 g canned chopped tomatoes

3¾ cups fish bouillon or vegetable bouillon

3 oz/85 g dried pasta shapes

12 oz/350 g firm white fish, such as cod, haddock, or hake

1 tbsp chopped fresh basil or oregano, or 1 tsp dried oregano

1 tsp grated lemon rind

1 tbsp cornstarch

1 tbsp water

salt and pepper

sprigs of fresh basil or oregano, to garnish

1   Heat the oil in a large pan. Add the onions and garlic and cook over low heat, stirring occasionally, for about 5 minutes, until softened. Add the zucchini and cook, stirring frequently, for 2–3 minutes.

2   Add the tomatoes and bouillon to the pan and bring to a boil. Add the pasta, bring back to a boil, lower the heat, and cover. Simmer for 5 minutes.

3   Skin and bone the fish, then cut it into chunks. Add to the pan with the basil or oregano, and the lemon rind, and simmer gently for 5 minutes, until the fish is opaque and flakes easily (take care not to overcook it). The pasta should be tender, but still firm to the bite.

4   Blend the cornstarch and water to a smooth paste and stir into the stew. Cook gently for 2 minutes, stirring constantly, until thickened. Season to taste.

5   Ladle the stew into 4 warmed soup bowls. Garnish with sprigs of fresh basil or oregano and serve immediately.

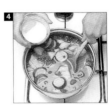

Lemon Spaghetti

Steaming vegetables helps preserve their nutritional content and lets them retain their bright, natural colors and crunchy texture.

NUTRITIONAL INFORMATION

Calories	133	Sugars	.........8g
Protein	.........8g	Fat	...........1g
Carbohydrate	...25g	Saturates	.....0.2g

🕙 10 mins   🕐 17 mins

SERVES 4

INGREDIENTS

8 oz/225 g celery root

2 medium carrots

2 medium leeks

1 small red bell pepper

1 small yellow bell pepper

2 garlic cloves

1 tsp celery seeds

1 tbsp lemon juice

10½ oz/300 g spaghetti

salt

chopped celery leaves, to garnish

LEMON DRESSING

1 tsp finely grated lemon rind

1 tbsp lemon juice

4 tbsp lowfat plain yogurt

salt and pepper

2 tbsp chopped fresh chives

1 Peel the celery root and carrots, cut into thin batons, and place in a bowl. Trim and slice the leeks, rinse under cold running water to flush out any trapped dirt, then shred finely. Halve, seed, and slice the bell peppers. Peel and thinly slice the garlic.

2 Add all of the vegetables to the bowl with the celery root and the carrots.

Toss the vegetables with the celery seeds and lemon juice.

3 Bring a large pan of lightly salted water to a boil. Add the pasta, bring back to a boil, and cook for 8–10 minutes, until tender but still firm to the bite. Drain and keep warm.

4 Meanwhile, bring another large pan of water to a boil, put the vegetables in a steamer, and place over the boiling water. Cover and steam for 6–7 minutes or until tender.

5 Meanwhile, combine all the ingredients for the lemon dressing.

6 Transfer the spaghetti and vegetables to a warmed serving bowl and mix with the dressing. Garnish with chopped celery leaves and serve.

Pasta Provençale

A combination of vegetables tossed in a tomato dressing, served on a bed of assorted salad greens, makes a tasty entrée or an appetizing side dish.

NUTRITIONAL INFORMATION

Calories	197	Sugars	.........5g
Protein	........10g	Fat	...........5g
Carbohydrate	...30g	Saturates	.......1g

 10 mins   15 mins

SERVES 4

INGREDIENTS

2 cups penne

1 tbsp olive oil

1 oz/25 g pitted black olives, drained and sliced into rings

1 oz/25 g dry-pack sun-dried tomatoes, soaked, drained, and chopped

14 oz/400 g canned artichoke hearts, drained and halved

4 oz/115 g baby zucchini, trimmed and sliced

4 oz/115 g baby plum tomatoes, halved

assorted young salad greens

salt and pepper

shredded basil leaves, to garnish

DRESSING

4 tbsp sieved tomatoes

2 tbsp lowfat unsweetened yogurt

1 tbsp unsweetened orange juice

small bunch fresh basil, shredded

1 Cook the penne according to the directions on the package. Do not overcook the pasta—it should be tender but still firm to the bite. Drain well and return to the pan. Stir in the olive oil, olives, sun-dried tomatoes, and seasoning. Let cool.

2 Gently mix the artichokes, zucchini, and plum tomatoes into the cooked pasta. Arrange the salad greens in a serving bowl.

3 To make the dressing, mix all the ingredients together and toss into the vegetables and pasta.

4 Spoon the mixture on top of the salad leaves and garnish with shredded basil leaves.

VARIATION
Try making this dish with other pasta shapes, or a mixture—look out for farfalle (bows) and rotelle (spoked wheels).

Pasta & Anchovy Sauce

This is an ideal dish for cooks in a hurry because it can be prepared in minutes from pantry ingredients.

NUTRITIONAL INFORMATION

Calories	712	Sugars	. . . . .4g
Protein	. . . . .25g	Fat	. . . . .34g
Carbohydrate	. . .81g	Saturates	. . . . .8g

🍲 10 mins   🕐 20 mins

SERVES 4

I N G R E D I E N T S

6 tbsp olive oil

2 garlic cloves, crushed

2¼ oz/60 g canned anchovy fillets, drained

1 lb/450 g dried spaghetti

2¼ oz/60 g pesto sauce (available ready-made from many stores)

2 tbsp finely chopped fresh oregano

3¼ oz/90 g grated Parmesan cheese, plus extra to garnish (optional)

salt and pepper

sprigs of fresh oregano, to garnish

1 Reserve 1 tablespoon of the oil and heat the remainder in a small pan. Add the garlic and cook for 3 minutes.

2 Lower the heat, stir in the anchovies, and cook, stirring occasionally, until the anchovies have disintegrated.

3 Bring a large pan of lightly salted water to a boil. Add the spaghetti and the remaining olive oil and cook for 8–10 minutes, or until just tender but still firm to the bite.

4 Add the pesto sauce and chopped fresh oregano to the garlic and anchovy mixture, and then season with pepper to taste.

5 Drain the spaghetti, using a slotted spoon, and transfer to a warm serving dish. Pour the pesto sauce over the spaghetti and then sprinkle over the grated Parmesan cheese.

6 Garnish with sprigs of fresh oregano, and extra Parmesan cheese, if using.

COOK'S TIP

If you find canned anchovies too salty, soak them in a saucer of cold milk for 5 minutes, drain, and pat dry with paper towels before using. The milk absorbs the salt.

Cream & Sage Tagliarini

This simple, creamy, bleu cheese and fresh sage sauce on freshly cooked tagliarini pasta is a classic Italian recipe.

NUTRITIONAL INFORMATION

Calories 880	Sugars 3g	
Protein 35g	Fat 49g	
Carbohydrate ...79g	Saturates 27g	

 10 mins   25 mins

SERVES 4

I N G R E D I E N T S

2 tbsp butter

2 cups coarsely crumbled Gorgonzola cheese

⅔ cup heavy cream

2 tbsp dry white wine

1 tsp cornstarch

4 sprigs of fresh sage, finely chopped

salt and white pepper

14 oz/400 g dried tagliarini

2 tbsp olive oil

 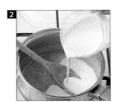 

1 Melt the butter in a heavy pan. Stir in 1½ cups of the Gorgonzola cheese and then melt, over low heat, for about 2 minutes.

2 Add the cream, wine, and cornstarch and beat with a whisk until all the ingredients are fully incorporated.

3 Stir in the sage and season to taste with salt and white pepper. Bring to a boil over low heat, whisking constantly, until the sauce thickens. Remove from the heat and set aside.

4 Bring a large pan of lightly salted water to a boil. Add the tagliarini and half of the olive oil. Cook the pasta for 12–14 minutes, or until just tender, then drain thoroughly and toss in the remaining olive oil. Transfer the pasta to a serving dish and keep warm.

5 Return the pan containing the sauce to the stove and reheat over low heat, whisking constantly. Spoon the Gorgonzola sauce over the tagliarini, generously sprinkle over the remaining cheese, and serve immediately.

COOK'S TIP

When buying Gorgonzola, always check that it is creamy yellow with delicate green veining. Avoid hard or discolored cheese. If you find Gorgonzola too strong or rich, you could use Danish bleu cheese instead.

Spicy Chorizo Vermicelli

Simple and quick to make, this spicy dish will set the taste buds tingling, with its exotic mushrooms, chiles, and anchovies.

NUTRITIONAL INFORMATION

Calories 672   Sugars 1g
Protein . . . . 16g   Fat 27g
Carbohydrate . . . 90g   Saturates 6g

 5 mins   10–12 mins

SERVES 6

INGREDIENTS

1 lb 8 oz/680 g dried vermicelli

½ cup olive oil

2 garlic cloves

4½ oz/125 g chorizo, sliced

8 oz/225 g exotic mushrooms

3 fresh red chiles, chopped

salt and pepper

2 tbsp freshly grated Parmesan cheese

anchovy fillets, to garnish

1 Bring a large pan of lightly salted water to a boil. Add the vermicelli and 1 tablespoon of the oil, and cook al dente, in other words tender but still firm to the bite. Drain and place on a large, heated plate to keep warm.

2 Meanwhile heat the remaining oil in a large skillet. Add the garlic and cook for 1 minute. Add the chorizo and exotic mushrooms and cook for 4 minutes, then add the chopped chiles and cook for another minute.

3 Pour the chorizo and wild mushroom mixture over the vermicelli, and season with a little salt and pepper. Sprinkle over freshly grated Parmesan cheese, garnish with anchovy fillets, and serve immediately.

VARIATION

Fresh sardines may be used in this recipe in place of the anchovies. However, ensure that you gut and clean the sardines and remove the backbone before using them.

Pasta & Chili Tomatoes

The pappardelle and vegetables in this dish are tossed in a delicious chili and tomato sauce for a quick and economical meal.

NUTRITIONAL INFORMATION

Calories	353	Sugars	.........7g
Protein	........10g	Fat	..........24g
Carbohydrate	...26g	Saturates	.......4g

 15 mins 20 mins

SERVES 4

I N G R E D I E N T S

10 oz/280 g dried pappardelle

3 tbsp peanut oil

2 garlic cloves, crushed

2 shallots, sliced

8 oz/225 g green beans, sliced

3½ oz/100 g cherry tomatoes, halved

1 tsp chili flakes

4 tbsp crunchy peanut butter

⅔ cup coconut milk

1 tbsp tomato paste

sliced scallions, to garnish

1 Bring a large pan of lightly salted water to a boil. Add the pappardelle, bring back to a boil, and cook for 8–10 minutes, until tender but still firm to the bite. Drain thoroughly and set aside.

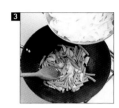

2 Meanwhile, heat the peanut oil in a large, heavy skillet or preheated wok. Add the garlic and shallots and stir-fry for 1 minute.

3 Add the green beans and drained pasta to the pan and stir-fry for 5 minutes. Add the halved cherry tomatoes and mix well.

4 Combine the chili flakes, peanut butter, coconut milk, and tomato paste. Pour the chili mixture into the pan, toss well to combine, and heat through.

5 Transfer to warm serving dishes and garnish with scallion slices. Serve immediately.

VARIATION

Add slices of chicken or beef to the recipe and stir-fry with the beans and pasta in step 3 for a more substantial meal.

Pasta & Chicken Medley

Strips of cooked chicken are tossed with colored pasta, grapes, and carrot sticks in a pesto-flavored dressing.

NUTRITIONAL INFORMATION	
Calories 609	Sugars 11g
Protein 26g	Fat 38g
Carbohydrate ...45g	Saturates 6g

30 mins   10 mins

SERVES 2

INGREDIENTS

generous 1–1⅓ cups dried pasta shapes,
    such as twists or bows

2 tbsp mayonnaise

2 tsp bottled pesto sauce

1 tbsp sour cream

6 oz/175g cooked skinless, boneless
    chicken meat

1–2 celery stalks

4½ oz/125 g black grapes
    (preferably seedless)

1 large carrot

salt and pepper

celery leaves, to garnish

FRENCH DRESSING

1 tsp wine vinegar

1 tbsp extra-virgin olive oil

salt and pepper

1 To make the French dressing, whisk all the ingredients together until smooth.

2 Bring a large pan of lightly salted water to a boil. Add the pasta, bring back to a boil, and cook for 8–10 minutes, until tender but still firm to the bite. Drain thoroughly, rinse, and drain again. Transfer to a bowl and mix in the French dressing while still hot, then set aside until cold.

3 Combine the mayonnaise, pesto sauce, and sour cream in a bowl and season to taste with salt and pepper.

4 Cut the chicken into thin strips. Cut the celery diagonally into thin slices. Reserve a few grapes for garnish, halve the rest, and remove any seeds. Cut the carrot into narrow julienne strips.

5 Add the chicken, celery, halved grapes, carrot, and mayonnaise mixture to the pasta and toss thoroughly. Taste and adjust the seasoning, adding more salt and pepper if necessary.

6 Arrange the pasta mixture on 2 plates and garnish with the reserved black grapes and the celery leaves.

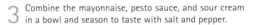
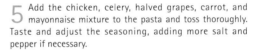

Pasta with Cheese & Broccoli

Some of the simplest and most satisfying dishes are made with pasta, such as this delicious combination of tagliatelle with two-cheese sauce.

NUTRITIONAL INFORMATION

Calories 624	Sugars 2g	
Protein 22g	Fat 45g	
Carbohydrate . . .34g	Saturates 28g	

 5 mins   15 mins

SERVES 4

INGREDIENTS

10½ oz/300 g dried tagliatelle tricolore
(orange, white, and green pasta ribbons)

8 oz/225 g broccoli, broken into
small florets

12 oz/350 g mascarpone cheese

4½ oz/125 g bleu cheese, chopped

1 tbsp chopped fresh oregano

salt and pepper

2 tbsp butter

sprigs of fresh oregano, to garnish

freshly grated Parmesan, to serve

1 Cook the tagliatelle in plenty of boiling salted water for 8–10 minutes, or until just tender.

2 Meanwhile, cook the broccoli florets in a small amount of lightly salted, boiling water. Try to avoid overcooking the broccoli, so that it retains much of its color and texture.

3 Heat the mascarpone and bleu cheeses together gently in a large pan, until they are melted. Stir in the chopped oregano and season with salt and pepper to taste.

4 Drain the pasta thoroughly. Return it to the pan and add the butter, tossing the tagliatelle to coat it. Drain the broccoli well and add to the pasta with the sauce, tossing gently to mix.

5 Divide the pasta between 4 warmed serving plates. Garnish with sprigs of fresh oregano and serve with freshly grated Parmesan.

Tagliatelle with Mushrooms

This dish can be prepared in a moment—the intense flavors are sure to make this a popular recipe.

 15 mins   20 mins

SERVES 4

I N G R E D I E N T S

2 tbsp walnut oil

1 bunch scallions, sliced

2 garlic cloves, thinly sliced

8 oz/225 g mushrooms, sliced

1 lb/450 g fresh green and white tagliatelle

8 oz/225 g frozen chopped leaf spinach, thawed and drained

4 oz/115 g fullfat soft cheese with garlic and herbs

4 tbsp light cream

salt and pepper

½ cup chopped, unsalted pistachios

2 tbsp shredded fresh basil

sprigs of fresh basil, to garnish

fresh Italian bread, to serve

1 Gently heat the walnut oil in a wok or skillet and sauté the scallions and garlic for 1 minute, or until just soft. Add the mushrooms to the skillet, stir well, cover, and cook gently for 5 minutes, or until soft.

2 Meanwhile, bring a large pan of lightly salted water to a boil and cook the pasta for 3–5 minutes, or until just tender. Drain the pasta thoroughly and return to the pan.

3 Add the spinach to the mushrooms and heat through for 1–2 minutes. Add the cheese and let it melt slightly. Stir in the cream and continue to heat without letting it boil.

4 Pour the vegetable mixture over the pasta, season to taste, and mix well. Heat gently, stirring, for 2–3 minutes.

5 Transfer the pasta into a warmed serving bowl and sprinkle over the pistachios and shredded basil. Garnish with sprigs of fresh basil and serve with fresh Italian bread.

Spaghetti with Ricotta

This light pasta dish has a delicate flavor ideally suited to a summer lunch.

NUTRITIONAL INFORMATION

Calories	701	Sugars	12g
Protein	17g	Fat	40g
Carbohydrate	73g	Saturates	15g

5 mins   25 mins

SERVES 4

INGREDIENTS

12 oz/350 g dried spaghetti

3 tbsp butter

2 tbsp chopped fresh flatleaf parsley

1 cup freshly ground almonds

½ cup ricotta cheese

pinch of freshly grated nutmeg

pinch of ground cinnamon

⅔ cup crème fraîche

2 tbsp olive oil

½ cup hot chicken bouillon

1 tbsp pine nuts

salt and pepper

sprigs of fresh flatleaf parsley, to garnish

COOK'S TIP

Use 2 large forks to toss spaghetti or other long pasta, so that it is thoroughly coated with the sauce. Special spaghetti forks are available from some cookware departments and kitchen stores.

1 Bring a pan of lightly salted water to a boil. Add the spaghetti, bring back to a boil, and cook for 8–10 minutes, until tender but still firm to the bite.

2 Drain the pasta, return to the pan, and toss with the butter and chopped parsley. Set aside and keep warm.

3 To make the sauce, combine the ground almonds, ricotta cheese, nutmeg, cinnamon, and crème fraîche in a small pan and stir over low heat to a thick paste. Gradually stir in the oil. When the oil has been fully incorporated, gradually stir in the hot chicken bouillon, until smooth. Season to taste with pepper.

4 Transfer the spaghetti to a warm serving dish, pour the sauce over it, and toss together well (see Cook's Tip). Sprinkle over the pine nuts, garnish with the sprigs of fresh flatleaf parsley, and serve immediately.

Pasta with Nuts & Cheese

Simple and inexpensive, this tasty dish is fairly quick and easy to prepare, but looks and tastes very impressive.

10 mins   30 mins

SERVES 4

I N G R E D I E N T S

½ cup pine nuts

12 oz/350 g dried pasta shapes

2 zucchini, sliced

1 cup broccoli, broken into florets

1 cup fullfat soft cheese

⅔ cup milk

1 tbsp chopped fresh basil

4 oz/115 g white mushrooms, sliced

⅔ cup crumbled bleu cheese

salt and pepper

sprigs of fresh basil, to garnish

salad greens, to serve

4 Put the soft cheese into a pan and heat gently, stirring constantly. Add the milk and stir to mix. Add the basil and mushrooms and then cook gently for 2–3 minutes. Stir in the crumbled blue cheese and season to taste.

5 Drain the pasta and the vegetables and mix together. Pour over the cheese and mushroom sauce and add the pine nuts. Toss gently to mix. Garnish with basil sprigs and serve immediately with salad greens.

1 Scatter the pine nuts onto a cookie sheet and broil, turning occasionally, until lightly browned all over. Set aside.

2 Cook the pasta in plenty of boiling salted water for 8–10 minutes, or until it is just tender.

3 Meanwhile, cook the zucchini and broccoli in a small amount of boiling, lightly salted water for about 5 minutes, or until just tender.

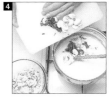

Pasta & Vegetable Sauce

This is a Mediterranean mixture of red bell peppers, garlic, and zucchini cooked in olive oil and tossed with pasta.

NUTRITIONAL INFORMATION

Calories	341	Sugars	.........8g
Protein	........13g	Fat	..........20g
Carbohydrate	...30g	Saturates	......8g

15 mins   20 mins

SERVES 4

INGREDIENTS

3 tbsp olive oil

1 onion, sliced

2 garlic cloves, chopped

3 red bell peppers, deseeded and cut into strips

3 zucchini, sliced

14 oz/400 g canned chopped tomatoes

3 tbsp sun-dried tomato paste

2 tbsp chopped fresh basil

8 oz/225 g fresh pasta spirals

1 cup grated Gruyère cheese

salt and pepper

fresh basil sprigs, to garnish

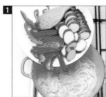  

COOK'S TIP
Be careful not to overcook fresh pasta–it should be *al dente* (retaining some 'bite'). It takes only a few minutes to cook as it is still full of moisture.

1 Heat the oil in a heavy-based pan or flameproof casserole. Add the onion and garlic and cook, stirring occasionally, until softened. Add the bell peppers and zucchini and fry for 5 minutes, stirring occasionally.

2 Add the tomatoes, sun-dried tomato paste, basil, and seasoning, cover, and cook for 5 minutes.

3 Meanwhile, bring a large pan of salted water to a boil and add the pasta. Stir and bring back to a boil. Reduce the heat slightly and cook, uncovered, for 3 minutes, or until just tender. Drain thoroughly and add to the vegetables. Toss gently to mix well.

4 Put the mixture into a large, shallow ovenproof dish and sprinkle over the cheese.

5 Cook under a preheated broiler for 5 minutes until the cheese is golden. Garnish with basil sprigs and serve.

Basil & Pine Nut Pasta

Pesto is delicious stirred into pasta, soups, and salad dressings, and is available in most supermarkets, but making your own gives a better flavor.

NUTRITIONAL INFORMATION

Calories 321	Sugars 1g
Protein 11g	Fat 17g
Carbohydrate . . .32g	Saturates 4g

 15 mins   10 mins

SERVES 4

I N G R E D I E N T S

about 40 fresh basil leaves, washed and patted dry with paper towels

3 garlic cloves, crushed

1 oz/25 g pine nuts

1¾ oz/50 g Parmesan cheese, finely grated

2–3 tbsp extra-virgin olive oil

salt and pepper

1 lb 8 oz/675 g fresh pasta or 12 oz/350 g dried pasta

1 Rinse the basil leaves and pat them dry with paper towels.

2 To make the pesto, put the basil leaves, garlic, pine nuts, and grated Parmesan into a food processor and blend for about 30 seconds, or until smooth. Alternatively, pound the ingredients by hand, using a mortar and pestle.

3 If you are using a food processor, keep the motor running and slowly add the olive oil. Alternatively, add the oil drop by drop while stirring briskly. Season with salt and pepper.

4 Meanwhile, cook the pasta in a pan of boiling water according to the instructions on the package, or until tender but still firm to the bite. Drain thoroughly.

5 Transfer the pasta to a serving plate and serve with the pesto. Toss to mix well and serve hot.

COOK'S TIP

You can store pesto in the refrigerator for about 4 weeks. Cover the surface of the pesto with olive oil before sealing the container or bottle, to prevent the basil from oxidizing and turning black.

Italian Tomato Pasta

In this dish, fresh tomatoes make a delicious Italian-style sauce, which goes particularly well with pasta.

NUTRITIONAL INFORMATION

Calories	304	Sugars	........8g
Protein	........15g	Fat	..........14g
Carbohydrate	...31g	Saturates	.......5g

 10 mins   25 mins

SERVES 2

I N G R E D I E N T S

1 tbsp olive oil

1 small onion, finely chopped

1–2 garlic cloves, crushed

12 oz/350 g tomatoes, peeled and chopped

2 tsp tomato paste

2 tbsp water

salt and pepper

10½–12 oz/300–350 g dried pasta shapes

3¼ oz/90 g lean bacon,
de-rinded and diced

1½ oz/40 g mushrooms, sliced

1 tbsp chopped fresh parsley or 1 tsp
chopped fresh cilantro

2 tbsp sour cream or plain fromage
frais (optional)

COOK'S TIP

Sour cream contains
18–20% fat, so if you are
following a lowfat diet you can
leave it out of this recipe or
substitute a lowfat alternative.

1 To make the tomato sauce, heat the oil in a pan and cook the onion and garlic gently, until soft.

2 Add the tomatoes, tomato paste, water, and salt and pepper to taste to the mixture in the pan and bring to a boil. Cover and simmer gently for 10 minutes.

3 Meanwhile, cook the pasta in a pan of boiling salted water for 8–10 minutes, or until just tender. Drain thoroughly and transfer to warm serving dishes.

4 Heat the bacon gently in a skillet until the fat runs, add the mushrooms, and continue cooking for 3–4 minutes. Drain off any excess fat.

5 Add the bacon and mushrooms to the tomato mixture, together with the parsley or cilantro and the sour cream or fromage frais, if using. Reheat and serve with the pasta.

Pasta with Green Vegetables

The different shapes and textures of the vegetables make a mouthwatering presentation in this light and summery dish.

NUTRITIONAL INFORMATION

Calories 517	Sugars 5g
Protein 17g	Fat 32g
Carbohydrate . . .42g	Saturates 18g

 10 mins   25 mins

SERVES 4

I N G R E D I E N T S

8 oz/225 g gemelli or other pasta shapes

1 tbsp olive oil

2 tbsp chopped fresh parsley

2 tbsp freshly grated Parmesan

salt and pepper

S A U C E

1 head of green broccoli, cut into florets

2 zucchini, sliced

8 oz/225 g asparagus spears, trimmed

4½ oz/125 g snow peas, trimmed

4½ oz/125 g frozen peas

2 tbsp butter

3 tbsp vegetable bouillon

5 tbsp heavy cream

large pinch of freshly grated nutmeg

1 Cook the pasta in a large pan of salted boiling water, adding the olive oil, for 8–10 minutes, or until tender. Drain the pasta in a colander, return to the pan, cover, and keep warm.

2 Steam the broccoli, zucchini, asparagus spears, and snow peas over a pan of boiling, salted water, until just beginning to soften. Remove from the heat and plunge into cold water to prevent them from cooking any farther. Drain and set aside.

3 Cook the peas in boiling, salted water for 3 minutes, then drain. Refresh in cold water and drain again.

4 Put the butter and vegetable bouillon in a pan over medium heat. Add all of the vegetables except for the asparagus spears and toss carefully with a wooden spoon to heat through, taking care not to break them up. Stir in the cream, let the sauce heat through, and season with salt and pepper, and nutmeg.

5 Transfer the pasta to a warmed serving dish and stir in the chopped parsley. Spoon over the sauce, and sprinkle on the freshly grated Parmesan. Arrange the asparagus spears in a pattern on top. Serve hot.

Spaghetti al Tonno

The classic Italian combination of pasta and tuna is enhanced in this recipe with a delicious parsley sauce.

NUTRITIONAL INFORMATION

Calories 1065	Sugars 3g	
Protein 27g	Fat 85g	
Carbohydrate 52g	Saturates 18g	

🥗 10 mins   🕐 15 mins

SERVES 4

I N G R E D I E N T S

7 oz/200 g canned tuna, drained

2¼ oz/60 g canned anchovies, drained

1⅛ cup olive oil

1 cup coarsely chopped flatleaf parsley

⅔ cup plain yogurt

1 lb/450 g dried spaghetti

2 tbsp butter

salt and pepper

black olives, to garnish

warm crusty bread, to serve

1 Remove any bones from the tuna. Put the tuna into a food processor or blender, with the anchovies, 1 cup of the olive oil, and the flatleaf parsley. Process until the sauce is very smooth.

2 Spoon the yogurt into the food processor or blender and process again for a few seconds to blend thoroughly. Season with salt and pepper to taste.

3 Bring a large pan of lightly salted water to a boil. Add the spaghetti and the remaining olive oil and cook for 8–10 minutes, or until tender but still firm to the bite.

4 Drain the spaghetti, return to the pan, and place over medium heat. Add the butter and toss well to coat. Spoon in the sauce and quickly toss into the spaghetti, mixing well using 2 forks.

5 Remove the pan from the heat and divide the spaghetti between warm individual serving plates. Garnish with olives and serve with warm crusty bread.

VARIATION

If desired, you could add 1–2 garlic cloves to the sauce, substitute ½ cup chopped fresh basil for half the parsley, and garnish with capers instead of black olives.

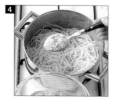

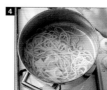

Poached Salmon with Penr

Fresh salmon and pasta in a mouthwatering lemon sauce—a marvelous summer evening treat.

NUTRITIONAL INFORMATION

Calories	968	Sugars	3g
Protein	59g	Fat	58g
Carbohydrate	49g	Saturates	19g

🍳 🍳

🥗 10 mins   🕐 30 mins

SERVES 4

I N G R E D I E N T S

4 fresh salmon steaks, about 9½ oz/ 275 g each

4 tbsp butter

¾ cup dry white wine

pinch of sea salt

8 peppercorns

sprig of fresh dill

sprig of fresh tarragon

1 lemon, sliced

1 lb/450 g dried penne

2 tbsp olive oil

lemon slices, and fresh watercress or young spinach leaves, to garnish

LEMON SAUCE

2 tbsp butter

3 tbsp all-purpose flour

⅔ cup warm milk

juice and finely grated zest of 2 lemons

2¼ oz/60 g watercress or young spinach leaves, chopped

salt and pepper

1 Place the salmon steaks in a large, nonstick pan. Add the butter, white wine, sea salt, peppercorns, dill, tarragon, and lemon. Cover, bring to a boil, and simmer for 10 minutes.

2 Using a spatula, carefully remove the salmon. Strain and reserve the cooking liquid. Remove and discard the salmon skin and central bones. Place on a warm dish, cover, and keep warm.

3 Meanwhile, bring a pan of salted water to a boil. Add the penne and half of the oil and cook for 8–10 minutes, or until tender but still firm to the bite. Drain and sprinkle over the remaining olive oil. Place on a warm serving dish, top with the salmon steaks, and keep warm.

4 To make the sauce, melt the butter and stir in the flour for 2 minutes. Stir in the milk and about 7 tablespoons of the reserved cooking liquid. Add the lemon juice and zest and cook, stirring, for another 10 minutes.

5 Add the watercress or spinach to the sauce, stir gently, and season to taste with salt and pepper.

6 Pour the sauce over the salmon and penne, garnish with slices of lemon and fresh watercress, and serve.

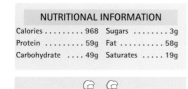

Pasta Carbonara

Lightly cooked eggs and pancetta are combined with cheese to make this rich, classic sauce.

15 mins   20 mins

SERVES 4

I N G R E D I E N T S

1 tbsp olive oil

3 tbsp butter

3½ oz/100 g pancetta or
  unsmoked bacon, diced

3 eggs, beaten

2 tbsp milk

1 tbsp thyme, stalks removed

salt and pepper

1 lb 8 oz/675 g fresh conchiglioni
  or 12 oz/350 g dried

1¾ oz/50 g Parmesan cheese, grated

1 Heat the oil and butter in a skillet, until the mixture is just beginning to froth.

2 Add the pancetta or bacon to the pan and cook for 5 minutes, or until browned all over.

3 Mix together the eggs and milk in a small bowl. Stir in the thyme and season to taste with salt and pepper.

4 Cook the pasta in a pan of boiling water about for 8–10 minutes, or until tender but still firm to the bite. Drain thoroughly.

5 Add the cooked, drained pasta to the skillet with the egg mixture and cook over high heat for 30 seconds, or until the eggs just begin to cook and set. Do not overcook the eggs or they will become rubbery.

6 Add half of the grated Parmesan cheese to the pan, stirring to combine.

7 Transfer the pasta to a serving plate, pour over the sauce and toss to mix well.

8 Sprinkle the rest of the grated Parmesan over the top and serve immediately.

VARIATION

For an extra-rich carbonara sauce, stir in 4 tablespoons of heavy cream with the eggs and milk in step 3. Follow the same cooking method.

Italian Chicken Spirals

These little foil pockets retain all the natural juices of the chicken while cooking conveniently over the pasta while it boils.

NUTRITIONAL INFORMATION

Calories	367	Sugars	.........1g
Protein	........33g	Fat	..........12g
Carbohydrate	...35g	Saturates	......2g

20 mins   20 mins

SERVES 4

INGREDIENTS

4 skinless, boneless chicken breasts

1 cup fresh basil leaves

2 tbsp hazelnuts

1 garlic clove, crushed

9 oz/250 g whole wheat pasta spirals

2 sun-dried tomatoes or fresh tomatoes

1 tbsp lemon juice

1 tbsp olive oil

1 tbsp capers

½ cup black olives

1 Beat the chicken breasts with a rolling pin to flatten evenly.

2 Place the basil and hazelnuts in a food processor and process until finely chopped. Mix with the garlic and salt and pepper to taste.

3 Spread the basil mixture over the chicken breasts and roll up from one short end to enclose the filling. Wrap the chicken rolls tightly in foil so that they hold their shape, then seal the ends well.

4 Bring a pan of lightly salted water to a boil and cook the pasta for 8–10 minutes or until tender, but still firm to the bite. Meanwhile, place the chicken pockets in a steamer or colander set over the pan, cover tightly, and steam for 10 minutes.

5 Using a sharp knife, dice the tomatoes.

6 Drain the pasta and return to the pan with the lemon juice, olive oil, tomatoes, capers, and olives. Heat through.

7 Pierce the chicken with a skewer to make sure that the juices run clear and not pink (this shows that the chicken is cooked through). Slice the chicken, arrange over the pasta, and serve.

COOK'S TIP
Sun-dried tomatoes have a wonderful, rich flavor but if they're unavailable, use fresh tomatoes instead.

Pasta Shells with Mussels

You can serve this aromatic seafood dish to members of your household and friends who have a love of garlic.

NUTRITIONAL INFORMATION

Calories	686	Sugars	........2g
Protein	........30g	Fat	.........45g
Carbohydrate	...36g	Saturates	.....27g

15 mins   25 mins

SERVES 4

INGREDIENTS

2 lb 12 oz/1.25 kg mussels

1 cup dry white wine

2 large onions, chopped

½ cup unsalted butter

6 large garlic cloves, finely chopped

5 tbsp chopped fresh parsley

1¼ cups heavy cream

14 oz/400 g dried pasta shells

1 tbsp olive oil

salt and pepper

warm crusty bread, to serve

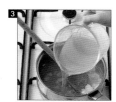

COOK'S TIP

Pasta shells are ideal because the sauce collects in the cavities and impregnates the pasta with flavor.

1 Scrub and debeard the mussels under cold running water. Discard any that do not close immediately when tapped sharply. Put the mussels into a large pan, together with the wine and half of the onions. Cover the pan and cook over medium heat, shaking the pan frequently, for 2–3 minutes, or until the shells open.

2 Remove the pan from the heat. Drain the mussels and reserve the cooking liquid. Discard any mussels that have not opened. Strain the cooking liquid through a clean cloth into a glass pitcher or bowl and reserve.

3 Melt the butter in a pan over medium heat. Add the remaining onion and cook until translucent. Stir in the garlic and cook for 1 minute. Gradually stir in the reserved cooking liquid. Stir in the parsley and cream and season to taste with salt and black pepper. Simmer over low heat.

4 Meanwhile, bring a large pan of lightly salted water to a boil. Add the pasta and olive oil and cook until just tender but still firm to the bite. Drain the pasta and return to the pan. Cover and keep warm.

5 Reserve a few mussels for the garnish and remove the remainder from their shells. Stir the shelled mussels into the cream sauce and warm briefly.

6 Transfer the pasta to a large, warm serving dish. Pour over the sauce and toss well to coat. Garnish with the reserved mussels and serve with warm, crusty bread.

Vermicelli with Clam Sauce

This is another cook-in-a-hurry recipe that transforms pantry ingredients into a dish with style.

NUTRITIONAL INFORMATION

Calories ....392 Sugars 2g
Protein ....23g Fat 15g
Carbohydrate ...37g Saturates 6g

5 mins   20 mins

SERVES 4

INGREDIENTS

14 oz/400 g vermicelli, spaghetti, or other long pasta

2 tbsp butter

salt

sprigs of fresh basil, to garnish

2 tbsp flaked Parmesan, to serve

SAUCE

1 tbsp olive oil

2 onions, chopped

2 garlic cloves, chopped

14 oz/400 g clams in brine

½ cup white wine

4 tbsp chopped parsley

½ tsp dried oregano

pinch of grated nutmeg

pepper

1 Bring a large pan of lightly salted water to a boil. Add the pasta, bring back to a boil, and cook for 8–10 minutes, until tender but still firm to the bite. Drain well, return to the pan, and add the butter. Cover and shake. Set the pan aside and keep warm.

2 To make the clam sauce, heat the oil in a pan. Add the onions and cook over low heat, stirring occasionally, for 5 minutes, until softened. Stir in the garlic and cook for another minute.

3 Strain the liquid from half of the clams and pour it into the pan. Strain the liquid from the remaining clams and discard. Reserve the clams.

4 Add the wine to the pan. Bring to simmering point, stirring constantly, and simmer for 3 minutes.

5 Add the clams and herbs to the pan and season to taste with nutmeg and pepper. Lower the heat and cook until the sauce is heated through.

6 Transfer the pasta to a warmed serving platter and pour the clam sauce over it.

7 Garnish with the basil and sprinkle on the Parmesan. Serve hot.

Pasta Vongole

Fresh clams are available from most good fish stores. If you prefer, use canned clams, which are less messy to eat but not so pretty to serve.

NUTRITIONAL INFORMATION	
Calories 410	Sugars 1g
Protein 39g	Fat 9g
Carbohydrate . . .39g	Saturates 1g

20 mins   20 mins

SERVES 4

I N G R E D I E N T S

1 lb 8 oz/675 g fresh clams or 10 oz/280 g canned clams, drained

2 tbsp olive oil

2 garlic cloves, finely chopped

14 oz/400 g mixed seafood, such as shrimp, squid, and mussels, thawed if frozen

⅔ cup white wine

⅔ cup fish bouillon

1 lb 8 oz/675 g fresh pasta or 12 oz/350 g dried pasta

2 tbsp chopped fresh tarragon

salt and pepper

1 If you are using fresh clams, scrub them clean and discard any that are already open.

2 Heat the oil in a large skillet. Add the garlic and the clams to the pan and cook for 2 minutes, shaking the pan to ensure that all of the clams are coated in the oil.

3 Add the remaining seafood to the pan and cook for an additional 2 minutes.

4 Pour the wine and bouillon over the mixed seafood and garlic and bring to a boil. Cover the pan, then lower the heat and let simmer for 8–10 minutes, or until the shells open. Discard any clams or mussels that do not open.

5 Meanwhile, cook the pasta in a pan of boiling water according to the instructions on the package, or until tender but still firm to the bite. Drain.

6 Stir the chopped tarragon into the sauce and season to taste with salt and pepper.

7 Transfer the pasta to a serving plate and then pour over the sauce.

VARIATION
Red clam sauce can be made by adding ½ cup of tomato paste to the sauce along with the bouillon in step 4. Follow the same cooking method.

Sea Bass with Olive Sauce

A favorite fish for chefs, the delicious sea bass is now becoming increasingly common in large food stores and fish stores for family meals.

NUTRITIONAL INFORMATION

Calories 877	Sugars 3g
Protein 50g	Fat 47g
Carbohydrate . . . 67g	Saturates 26g

10 mins   30 mins

SERVES 4

I N G R E D I E N T S

1 lb/450 g dried macaroni

1 tbsp olive oil

8 sea bass medallions, about
    4 oz/115 g each

S A U C E

2 tbsp butter

4 shallots, chopped

2 tbsp capers

1½ cups chopped pitted green olives

4 tbsp balsamic vinegar

1¼ cups fish bouillon

1¼ cups heavy cream

salt and pepper

juice of 1 lemon

T O   G A R N I S H

slices of fresh lemon

shredded leek

shredded carrot

1 To make the sauce, melt the butter in a skillet. Add the shallots and cook gently over low heat for 4 minutes. Add the capers and chopped olives and cook for another 3 minutes.

2 Stir in the balsamic vinegar and fish bouillon, bring to a boil, and reduce by half. Add the cream, stirring, and reduce again by half. Season to taste with salt and pepper and stir in the lemon juice. Remove the pan from the heat, set aside, and keep warm.

3 Bring a large pan of lightly salted water to a boil. Add the pasta and olive oil and cook for about 12 minutes, or until tender but still firm to the bite.

4 Meanwhile, lightly broil the sea bass medallions for 3–4 minutes on each side, until cooked through but still moist and delicate.

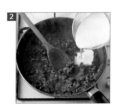

5 Drain the pasta thoroughly and transfer to large individual serving dishes. Top the pasta with the fish medallions and pour over the olive sauce. Garnish the sea bass with lemon slices, shredded leek, and shredded carrot, and serve immediately.

Spaghetti & Salmon Sauce

The smoked salmon in this recipe ideally complements the buckwheat spaghetti to give a very luxurious dish.

NUTRITIONAL INFORMATION

Calories 782	Sugars 3g	
Protein 20g	Fat 48g	
Carbohydrate ...48g	Saturates 27g	

10 mins   15 mins

SERVES 4

I N G R E D I E N T S

1 lb 2 oz/500 g buckwheat spaghetti

2 tbsp olive oil

3¼ oz/90 g feta cheese, crumbled

chopped fresh cilantro or parsley, to garnish

S A U C E

1¼ cups heavy cream

⅔ cup whiskey or brandy

4½ oz/125 g smoked salmon

large pinch of cayenne pepper

salt and pepper

2 tbsp chopped fresh cilantro or parsley

1 Put the spaghetti in a large pan of salted water, adding 1 tablespoon of the olive oil, and bring to a boil. Cook for 8–10 minutes, or until tender. Drain the pasta in a colander. Return the pasta to the pan, sprinkle over the remaining oil, cover, and shake the pan. Set aside and keep warm until required.

2 In separate small pans, heat the cream and the whiskey or brandy to simmering point. Do not let them boil.

3 Combine the cream with the whiskey or brandy.

4 Cut the smoked salmon into thin strips and then add them to the cream and whiskey mixture. Season with a little black pepper and cayenne pepper to taste, and then stir in the chopped fresh cilantro or parsley.

5 Transfer the spaghetti to a warmed serving dish, pour on the sauce, and toss thoroughly using two large forks. Scatter the crumbled cheese over the pasta and garnish with the chopped fresh cilantro or parsley. Serve at once.